The Friendship Brace

Creative Ideas to bec

Bracelet Craftsman.

Donna L. Matta

Contents   Pages

CHAPTER ONE

INTRODUCTION

1.1 The significance of friendship bracelets as tokens of love, friendship, and self-expression.

Friendship bracelets hold significant meaning as tokens of love, friendship, and self-expression. Here are some aspects that highlight their significance:

1. Symbol of Friendship: Friendship bracelets are traditionally exchanged as symbols of deep and enduring friendships. By giving or receiving a friendship bracelet, individuals express their love, care, and appreciation for one another. It serves as a tangible reminder of the special bond shared between friends.

2. Personalized Expression: Friendship bracelets offer a unique and personal way to express oneself. They can be customized with various colors, patterns, and designs that reflect the recipient's personality, interests, or shared memories. The act of creating and gifting a friendship bracelet demonstrates thoughtfulness and the effort put into understanding and honoring the recipient's individuality.

3. Connection and Unity: Friendship bracelets serve as a physical connection between friends, even when physically apart. Wearing a friendship bracelet can evoke a sense of closeness and unity, symbolizing the unbreakable bond between friends regardless of distance or time. It serves as a reminder that no matter where they are, their friendship remains strong.

4. Emotional Support and Encouragement: Friendship bracelets often hold sentimental value and can provide emotional support during challenging times. They serve as a source of comfort and encouragement, reminding individuals of the support and love they have from their friends. During difficult moments, the presence of a friendship bracelet can offer a sense of reassurance and strength.

5. Acts of Kindness and Generosity: Exchanging friendship bracelets can foster a culture of kindness and generosity. It encourages individuals to show appreciation and care for their friends through a thoughtful and handmade gift. The act of creating and sharing a friendship bracelet can bring joy and warmth to both the giver and the recipient, strengthening the bond between them.

6. Timeless Tradition: Friendship bracelets have been a part of various cultures and traditions for centuries. They have stood the test of time and continue to be cherished symbols of friendship in modern society. By embracing the tradition of friendship bracelets, individuals connect with a rich history of expressing friendship and love through handmade crafts.

7. Acts of Self-Care: Making and wearing friendship bracelets can also be an act of self-care. Engaging in a creative and mindful activity like bracelet making can promote relaxation, reduce stress, and enhance overall well-being. It allows individuals to express their creativity, focus on the present moment, and find joy in the process of creating something meaningful.

In summary, friendship bracelets hold immense significance as tokens of love, friendship, and self-expression. They represent the deep bonds shared between friends, provide a means for personalization and creative expression, and serve as physical reminders of support and unity. The tradition of friendship bracelets brings people together and fosters a sense of belonging, kindness, and appreciation in our relationships.

1.2 Overview of the materials and tools needed for creating friendship bracelets.

To create friendship bracelets, you will need a few essential materials and tools. Here is an overview of what you'll need:

1. Thread or Yarn: Choose thread or yarn in various colors to create your friendship bracelets. Embroidery floss is commonly used due to its vibrant colors and durability. You can also use cotton, nylon, silk, or hemp thread. Select colors that reflect your personal style or have special meaning for you and your friends.

2. Scissors: A pair of sharp scissors is essential for cutting the thread or yarn to the desired length. Make sure your scissors are suitable for cutting through the chosen material.

3. Tape or Clipboard: Use tape or a clipboard to hold the bracelet in place while you work. This helps maintain tension and prevents the bracelet from unraveling as you weave.

4. Beads and Charms (optional): Adding beads or charms to your friendship bracelets can enhance their visual appeal and personalize them further. Select beads or charms that fit the thread thickness and complement your chosen design.

5. Ruler or Measuring Tape: A ruler or measuring tape can help you determine the desired length for your friendship bracelet. It ensures a proper fit and allows for adjustments based on wrist size.

6. Closure Options: Consider how you want to secure your bracelet. Common closure options include braided ties, adjustable sliding knots, or clasps.

Choose a closure method that is both secure and easy to use.

7. Embroidery Needles (optional): If you plan to add embroidery or stitching to your friendship bracelets, you may need embroidery needles. These needles have sharp points and larger eyes to accommodate embroidery floss or thicker threads.

8. Design Tools (optional): You may find it helpful to use design tools such as graph paper or friendship bracelet pattern books. These tools can assist in creating intricate patterns or alphabets for personalized bracelets.

It's important to note that the specific materials and tools may vary based on the style of friendship bracelet you want to create. Different techniques and designs may require additional or specialized tools.

Consider starting with the basics mentioned above and gradually expand your collection as you explore different bracelet patterns and techniques. Experiment with different materials and colors to create unique and meaningful friendship bracelets.

1.3 Basic knotting techniques and terminology used in friendship bracelet making.

Friendship bracelet making involves several basic knotting techniques and associated terminology. Here are the fundamental knotting techniques commonly used in friendship bracelet making:

1. **Forward Knot:** Also known as a forward spiral or forward tie, this is the most basic knot used in friendship bracelet making. It is created by crossing one strand of thread over the other and pulling it through the loop formed, tightening the knot. The step by step process of making forward knot is shown below;

Step1: Assemble your materials (Friendship thread, Scissors & Clipboard)

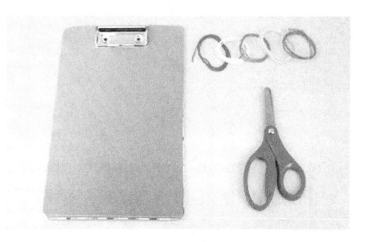

Step 2: Cut multiple strands of Friendship Thread to the desired length (say 22-24inches). Create a knot approximately 1 to 1 ½ inches away from the end by securing all five strands together.

Step 3: Attach the knot beneath the clipboard to keep it secure during the crafting process. Gently separate the strands, arranging them in the desired color order. To create a diagonal knot pattern, begin from the left side and designate the strands as follows: Strand 1 (pink), Strand 2 (orange), Strand 3 (yellow), Strand 4 (green), and Strand 5 (blue).

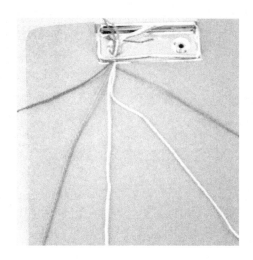

Step 4: Initiate the initial diagonal row by taking Strand 1 (pink) and crossing it over Strand 2 (orange), ensuring to leave a loop.

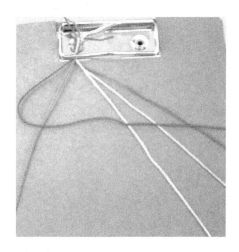

Step 5: Pass the end of Strand 1 (pink) under Strand 2 (orange).

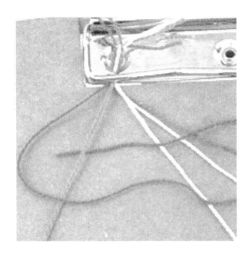

Step 6: Pull Strand 1 (pink) through the loop that was created in step 4.

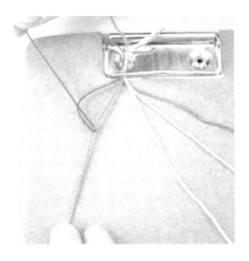

Step 7: While maintaining a firm grip on Strand 2 (orange), pull Strand 1 (pink) to create a knot. This knot is known as a spiral knot.

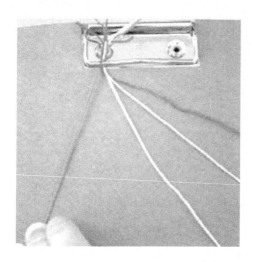

Step 8: Repeat Steps 4 to 7 with Strand 1 (pink) and Strand 2 (orange). By doing so, you will have completed two spiral knots.

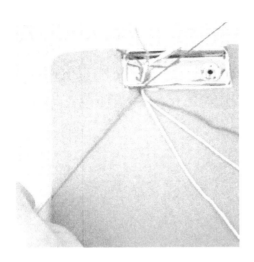

Step 9: Now, proceed to create the diagonal row by working across the strands. Take Strand 1 (pink) and Strand 3 (yellow), and repeat the spiral knot process described in Steps 4-7 twice. This will result in two pink spiral knots encircling Strand 3 (yellow).

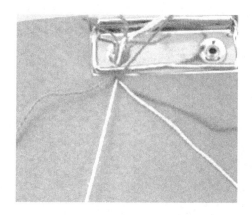

Step 10: Repeat the process of creating two spiral knots with Strand 1 (pink) and Strand 4 (green).

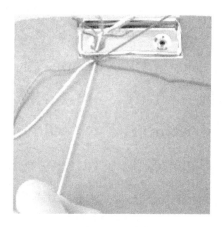

Step 11: Continue by repeating the steps for creating two spiral knots with Strand 1 (pink) and Strand 5 (blue).

Congratulations! You have successfully completed your first diagonal row.

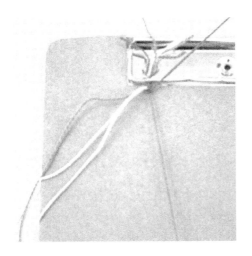

Step 12: To form the second diagonal row, refer to the revised labels for the strands in the new left-to-right order: Strand 1 is orange, Strand 2 is yellow, Strand 3 is green, Strand 4 is blue, and Strand 5 is pink. Repeat Steps 5 to 12 to create a diagonal row using the orange strand.

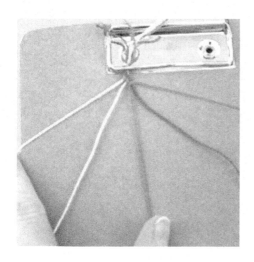

Step 13: Continue repeating Steps 5 to 12 with each leftmost strand in order to create a continuous diagonal knot pattern. This will allow you to progress through the entire row, maintaining the desired pattern as you go along.

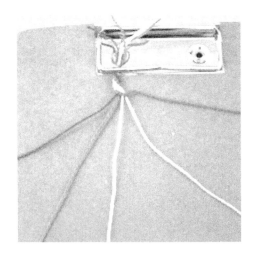

Step 14: Here is the final result

2. Backward Knot: Also known as a backward spiral or backward tie, this knot is the reverse of the forward knot. It is created by crossing one strand of thread over the other in the opposite direction and pulling it through the loop formed.

3. Double Forward Knot: This is an extension of the forward knot. It involves making two forward knots consecutively using the same strand of thread.

4. Double Backward Knot: Similar to the double forward knot, this knot involves making two backward knots consecutively using the same strand of thread.

5. Combination Knot: This knot is created by combining a forward knot and a backward knot in succession. It is commonly used to create chevron or V-shaped patterns.

6. Square Knot: The square knot consists of two half knots. It is created by crossing the left strand over the right strand and then crossing the right strand over the left strand. Repeat this process to create a series of square knots.

7. Half Hitch Knot: This knot is created by making a loop with one strand of thread and wrapping the other strand around it. Pull the end of the second strand through the loop, tightening the knot. Half hitch knots are often used in macramé techniques.

8. Sliding Knot: A sliding knot is used to create adjustable closures for friendship bracelets. It allows the bracelet to be easily loosened or tightened to fit the wrist. The sliding knot is typically created using a series of half hitch knots.

Understanding these basic knotting techniques will provide a solid foundation for creating a variety of friendship bracelet patterns and designs. Experiment with different combinations, knot sequences, and color arrangements to create unique and personalized bracelets.

CHAPTER TWO

CLASSIC SINGLE-COLOR BRACELET

2.1 Step-by-step instructions for creating a simple, single-color friendship bracelet using the forward knot technique.

Creating a simple, single-color friendship bracelet using the forward knot technique is a great way to start. Follow these step-by-step instructions:

Materials:

- Embroidery floss or thread in your desired color

- Scissors

Step 1: Measure and cut the thread

Start by measuring and cutting a piece of thread to your desired bracelet length. As a guideline, 60-70 inches (150-180 cm) is a common length for a standard bracelet.

Step 2: Prepare the thread

Fold the thread in half so that the ends meet, creating a loop at one end. This loop will be used for securing the bracelet later.

Step 3: Secure the loop

Take the looped end and create a knot close to the loop to secure it. This will serve as the starting point of your bracelet.

Step 4: Position the threads

Hold the knotted end of the bracelet in one hand, allowing the threads to hang freely. You will have two sets of threads: a set on the left and a set on the right.

Step 5: Start knotting

Take the left thread and cross it over the right thread, creating a loop.

Step 6: Thread through the loop

Take the left thread and pass it through the loop created in Step 5 from the back to the front.

Step 7: Tighten the knot

Hold the right thread and the loop created by the left thread. Gently pull the left thread to tighten the knot. Ensure the knot is snug but not overly tight.

Step 8: Repeat the forward knot

Repeat Steps 5-7, but this time, start with the right thread crossing over the left thread. Pass the right thread through the loop and tighten the knot. This completes one forward knot.

Step 9: Continue knotting

Continue repeating the forward knot (left thread over right thread, right thread over left thread) until you reach your desired bracelet length. Regularly check the length by wrapping the bracelet around your wrist.

Step 10: Finishing the bracelet

Once you reach your desired length, tie a knot at the end of the bracelet to secure the threads. Trim any excess thread, leaving a small tail.

Step 11: Securing the bracelet

Take the looped end of the bracelet created in Step 2. Slide it through the knot at the other end of the bracelet. Pull the loop gently to secure the bracelet around your wrist.

2.2 Tips for choosing thread colors and achieving a neat and consistent pattern.

Choosing thread colors and achieving a neat and consistent pattern in friendship bracelets can greatly enhance their visual appeal. Here are some tips to consider:

1. Color Selection:

- **Consider the recipient's preferences:** Choose colors that reflect the recipient's favorite colors or their personal style.

- **Harmonious color combinations:** Select colors that complement each other well. Look for color wheels or online resources that can guide you in choosing complementary, analogous, or monochromatic color schemes.

- **Contrast for visibility:** If you want the pattern to stand out, choose thread colors with strong contrast. For example, light and dark shades, or complementary colors.

2. Planning and Design:

- **Sketch or plan your pattern:** Before starting, visualize or sketch the pattern you want to create. This will help you organize the colors and ensure a consistent design throughout the bracelet.

- **Consider symmetry:** If you're aiming for a symmetrical design, make sure you mirror the colors and patterns on both sides of the bracelet.

3. Consistent Knotting and Tension:

- **Maintain even tension:** Keep the tension consistent as you knot the threads to ensure an even and neat pattern. Too loose or too tight knots can affect the appearance of the bracelet.

- **Use a clipboard or tape:** Secure the bracelet to a clipboard or use tape to hold it in place while you work. This helps maintain tension and prevents the bracelet from unraveling or becoming uneven.

4. Practice and Patience:

- **Start with simple patterns:** Begin with simple patterns to familiarize yourself with the knotting technique and achieve consistency.

- **Take your time:** Pay attention to each knot and take your time to ensure accuracy. Rushing can lead to mistakes and an uneven pattern.

5. Attention to Detail:

- **Double-check color placement:** Before starting a new row or section, ensure that the correct color is in the desired position. This helps maintain the pattern and prevents mistakes.

- **Trim excess thread:** Regularly trim excess thread to keep the bracelet neat and avoid tangling.

6. Experiment and Have Fun:

- Don't be afraid to experiment: Explore different color combinations, patterns, and techniques. Friendships bracelets are all about creativity and personal expression.

- Learn from mistakes: If you make a mistake or encounter an inconsistency, don't be discouraged. Learn from it and use it as an opportunity to improve your skills.

Remember, achieving a neat and consistent pattern may require practice and patience. The more you create, the better you'll become at selecting colors and creating intricate designs. Enjoy the process and embrace the uniqueness of each friendship bracelet you make!

2.3 Variations and ideas for adding embellishments, such as beads or charms.

Adding embellishments like beads or charms to friendship bracelets can elevate their visual appeal and make them more personalized. Here are some variations and ideas for incorporating embellishments:

1. Beaded Accents:

- **Add beads between knots:** Instead of knotting the thread continuously, insert beads between knots at regular intervals. This creates a decorative pattern with beads.

- **Use different sizes and shapes:** Experiment with beads of various sizes, shapes, and colors to create unique designs. Mix and match different bead combinations for a playful or sophisticated look.

- Use seed beads as spacers: String small seed beads onto the threads before knotting. These beads can act as spacers and create a delicate pattern within the bracelet.

2. Charms and Pendants:

- Attach charms to the closure: Use jump rings or thread the charm directly onto the closure loop to add a decorative element to the bracelet's closure.

- Thread charms into the pattern: Incorporate charms into the design by threading them onto the threads at specific points in the pattern. This allows the charm to be showcased within the bracelet's pattern.

3. Letter or Initial Beads:

- **Personalize with initials:** Include letter beads or alphabet beads to spell out initials or names of the recipient or the wearer of the bracelet. Place the letter beads strategically within the pattern to create a personalized touch.

- **Create words or messages:** Use letter beads to spell out words or inspirational messages. Combine them with other beads or knot patterns to enhance the design.

4. Mixed Materials:

- Combine different materials: Experiment with mixing different materials such as beads, threads, leather cords, or ribbons. This creates a dynamic and eclectic look for the bracelet.

- Wrap threads around larger beads: Wrap threads around larger beads or stones to create a unique focal point. This technique adds texture and visual interest to the bracelet.

5. Tassels:

- Add tassels to the closure: Attach small tassels made of thread or embroidery floss to the closure loop. This adds a bohemian or playful touch to the bracelet.

- Incorporate tassels within the pattern: Create tassels by grouping multiple strands of thread and tying them together. Attach these tassels at specific points within the bracelet's pattern.

Remember to consider the size and weight of the embellishments to ensure they are suitable for the bracelet's design and won't affect the bracelet's comfort or durability. Be creative and explore different combinations to add your personal touch and create unique friendship bracelets with embellishments.

CHAPTER THREE

CHEVRON BRACELET

3.1 Detailed guide for weaving a Chevron pattern friendship bracelet with two or more colors.

Creating a Chevron pattern friendship bracelet with two or more colors is a popular choice for its vibrant and visually appealing design. Follow this step-by-step guide to weave a Chevron pattern bracelet:

Materials:

- Embroidery floss or thread in two or more colors (e.g., Color A and Color B)

- Scissors

- Clipboard or tape (optional, for securing the bracelet)

Step 1: Prepare the threads

Cut two strands of thread in each color, measuring approximately 60-70 inches (150-180 cm) in length. Fold each strand in half and align the ends, so you have two sets of folded threads.

Step 2: Secure the threads

Take one set of Color A threads and one set of Color B threads. Align the folded ends and tie a knot at the folded end, leaving a small loop. This loop will serve as the starting point of your bracelet.

Step 3: Position the threads

Hold the knotted end of the bracelet in one hand, allowing the threads to hang freely. You will have two sets of threads: a set on the left (Color A) and a set on the right (Color B).

Step 4: Start the pattern

Take the outermost thread of Color A from the left side and make a forward knot over the adjacent thread of Color B on the right side. This creates a diagonal line with the Color A thread now on the right side.

Step 5: Repeat the knotting sequence

Continuing with the outermost thread of Color A on the right side, make a forward knot over the adjacent thread of Color B on the left side. This brings the Color A thread back to the left side.

Step 6: Repeat Steps 4 and 5

Continue repeating Steps 4 and 5 alternately, always working with the outermost thread on each side. This creates a V-shape pattern with alternating colors.

Step 7: Add additional colors (optional)

To add more colors to the Chevron pattern, introduce a new color by folding a new set of threads and knotting them with the existing set. Continue the knotting sequence, alternating colors as desired.

Step 8: Continue the pattern

Repeat Steps 4 to 7 until you reach your desired bracelet length. Regularly check the length by wrapping the bracelet around your wrist.

Step 9: Finishing the bracelet

Once you reach your desired length, tie a knot at the end of the bracelet to secure the threads. Trim any excess thread, leaving a small tail.

Step 10: Secure the bracelet (optional)

If desired, secure the bracelet to a clipboard or use tape to hold it in place while you work. This helps maintain tension and prevents the bracelet from unraveling or becoming uneven.

3.2 Instructions for creating a Chevron design using both forward and backward knots.

Creating a Chevron design using both forward and backward knots adds texture and depth to the friendship bracelet. Follow these step-by-step instructions to weave a Chevron pattern using both forward and backward knots:

Materials:

- Embroidery floss or thread in two or more colors (e.g., Color A and Color B)

- Scissors

- Clipboard or tape (optional, for securing the bracelet)

Step 1: Prepare the threads

Cut two strands of thread in each color, measuring approximately 60-70 inches (150-180 cm) in length. Fold each strand in half and align the ends, so you have two sets of folded threads.

Step 2: Secure the threads

Take one set of Color A threads and one set of Color B threads. Align the folded ends and tie a knot at the folded end, leaving a small loop. This loop will serve as the starting point of your bracelet.

Step 3: Position the threads

Hold the knotted end of the bracelet in one hand, allowing the threads to hang freely. You will have two sets of threads: a set on the left (Color A) and a set on the right (Color B).

Step 4: Start the pattern with a backward knot

Take the outermost thread of Color A from the left side and make a backward knot over the adjacent thread of Color B on the right side. This creates a diagonal line with the Color A thread now on the right side.

Step 5: Continue with a forward knot

Take the outermost thread of Color B on the right side and make a forward knot over the adjacent thread of Color A on the left side. This brings the Color B thread back to the left side.

Step 6: Repeat the knotting sequence

Continue repeating the knotting sequence: backward knot with Color A, followed by a forward knot with Color B.

Step 7: Create the Chevron pattern

As you repeat the knotting sequence, the backward knots with Color A and the forward knots with Color B will create a V-shape pattern. Continue alternating between backward knots and forward knots to form the Chevron design.

Step 8: Add additional colors (optional)

To add more colors to the Chevron pattern, introduce a new color by folding a new set of threads and knotting them with the existing set. Continue the knotting sequence, alternating colors as desired.

Step 9: Continue the pattern

Repeat Steps 4 to 8 until you reach your desired bracelet length. Regularly check the length by wrapping the bracelet around your wrist.

Step 10: Finishing the bracelet

Once you reach your desired length, tie a knot at the end of the bracelet to secure the threads. Trim any excess thread, leaving a small tail.

Step 11: Secure the bracelet (optional)

If desired, secure the bracelet to a clipboard or use tape to hold it in place while you work. This helps maintain tension and prevents the bracelet from unraveling or becoming uneven.

3.3 Tips for experimenting with color combinations and incorporating gradients or ombre effects.

Experimenting with color combinations and incorporating gradients or ombre effects in friendship bracelets can add visual interest and create unique designs. Here are some tips to help you achieve stunning color effects:

1. Choose complementary colors:

Select colors that are opposite each other on the color wheel to create a high-contrast and vibrant look. For example, pair blue with orange or yellow with purple.

2. Use analogous colors: Choose colors that are adjacent to each other on the

color wheel for a harmonious and cohesive color scheme. This creates a smooth transition between shades.

3. Create a gradient effect: To achieve a gradient effect, select a color palette that includes different shades of the same color. Start with the darkest shade and gradually transition to lighter shades. This can be done by gradually changing thread colors or by blending colors together.

4. Blend colors: Combine two or more thread colors to create a blended or marbled effect. This can be done by tying different colors together and using them as one thread or by twisting two or more threads together before knotting.

5. Ombre effect: Create an ombre effect by using threads in different shades of the same color. Start with the darkest shade at one end of the bracelet and gradually transition to lighter shades as you progress. This can be achieved by using threads in different shades or by gradually adding or removing threads of a lighter or darker shade.

6. Consider thread thickness: When incorporating gradients or ombre effects, consider using threads of different thicknesses. Thicker threads will create a bolder and more pronounced effect, while thinner threads will create a more subtle transition.

7. Test color combinations: Before starting your bracelet, take some time to test different color combinations and effects on a small piece of string or cardboard. This allows you to see how the colors blend together and make adjustments if needed.

8. Experiment with pattern variations: Combine different color combinations with various knotting patterns and techniques. Try alternating colors within the pattern or creating color blocks to enhance the overall design.

9. Seek inspiration: Look for inspiration in nature, fashion, or other crafts to discover unique color combinations and effects. Pinterest, craft blogs, and color palette websites can provide inspiration for your friendship bracelet projects.

Remember, the key is to have fun and let your creativity guide you. Don't be afraid to try new color combinations and techniques. Each combination will result in a one-of-a-kind friendship bracelet that reflects your personal style and creativity. Enjoy the process of experimenting with colors and creating beautiful and meaningful bracelets for yourself and your friends.

CHAPTER FOUR

ALPHA PATTERN BRACELET

4.1 Introduction to alpha patterns, which allow you to weave letters or words into your bracelet.

Alpha patterns are a popular technique used in friendship bracelet making to incorporate letters or words into your designs. These patterns allow you to weave names, initials, messages, or any other text into your bracelets, adding a personal and meaningful touch. Here's an introduction to alpha patterns and how to use them:

1. Understanding the Grid:

Alpha patterns are created using a grid, where each cell represents a knot. The grid consists of rows and columns, with each cell indicating the color and position of the knot.

2. Selecting an Alpha Pattern:

There are numerous resources available online that provide free or downloadable alpha patterns. You can find websites, forums, or even mobile apps dedicated to sharing and creating these patterns. Choose a pattern that suits your desired text and bracelet width.

3. Preparing the Thread:

To create the alpha pattern, you'll need threads in different colors. Choose thread colors that provide good contrast with the background color of your bracelet. Cut the threads into suitable lengths, usually around 60-70 inches (150-180 cm) each.

4. Transferring the Pattern:

Place the alpha pattern grid in front of you or secure it to a clipboard or surface. Take your base bracelet threads (the ones you'll use for the background) and knot them as usual, leaving a short tail.

5. Following the Pattern:

Using the alpha pattern grid as your guide, identify the color and position of each knot for the letters or words you want to create. Pay attention to the thread colors indicated in the grid and the corresponding cells. Start with the first row of the pattern and work your way down, knotting the corresponding threads to form the desired letters.

6. Knotting Techniques:

To weave the letters or words, you'll use knotting techniques such as forward knots, backward knots, or double knots. The choice of technique depends on the pattern and design. Follow the instructions provided in the pattern or refer to the specific knotting techniques mentioned in earlier sections.

7. Transitioning between Letters:

When moving from one letter to the next, keep in mind that you may need to carry the threads across or knot them off before starting the next letter. This helps maintain a neat and organized appearance.

8. Completing the Bracelet:

Once you've completed the alpha pattern, continue knotting the base threads to complete the rest of the bracelet. You can use a single color or incorporate additional patterns or designs to complement the alpha pattern.

Using alpha patterns allows you to personalize your friendship bracelets with names, messages, or meaningful words. It requires a bit of patience and attention to detail, but the end result is a beautiful and unique bracelet that carries a special significance. Experiment with different patterns, thread colors, and bracelet designs to create personalized and cherished pieces for yourself and your friends.

4.2 Instructions for following an alpha pattern chart to create personalized messages or initials.

Following an alpha pattern chart allows you to create personalized messages or initials in your friendship bracelets. Here are step-by-step instructions to help you successfully use an alpha pattern chart:

Materials:

- Alpha pattern chart

- Base threads (background color)

- Thread colors for the letters or initials

- Scissors

- Clipboard or tape (optional, for securing the bracelet)

Step 1: Choose an Alpha Pattern Chart

Select an alpha pattern chart that corresponds to the message or initials you want to create. You can find a variety of alpha patterns online or in crafting books. Make sure the chart is clear and easy to read.

Step 2: Prepare the Base Threads

Cut the base threads to the desired length, usually around 60-70 inches (150-180 cm). These threads will form the background of your bracelet. Tie a knot at one end of the threads, leaving a small loop.

Step 3: Understand the Alpha Pattern Chart

Familiarize yourself with the symbols and colors used in the alpha pattern chart. Each symbol represents a specific thread color and knotting direction. Take note of the key or legend provided with the chart to understand the color codes and symbols.

Step 4: Secure the Alpha Pattern Chart

Place the alpha pattern chart in front of you, or secure it to a clipboard or surface for easy reference. Make sure the chart is positioned in a way that you can easily see and follow the symbols and instructions.

Step 5: Start Knotting

Refer to the first symbol or letter in the alpha pattern chart. Identify the corresponding thread color and knotting direction. Hold the base threads with the background color in one hand and the thread color for the letter or initial in the other hand.

Step 6: Follow the Chart Row by Row

Begin knotting according to the chart, following each row from left to right or right to left, depending on the instructions. Use the appropriate knotting technique (e.g., forward knot, backward knot) indicated in the chart for each symbol.

Step 7: Transition between Letters or Initials

If your alpha pattern chart includes multiple letters or initials, pay attention to the instructions for transitioning between them. Follow any indicated arrows or lines in the chart to know when to start and stop each letter or initial.

Step 8: Maintain Consistent Tension

As you knot each symbol, ensure consistent tension in the threads to create a neat and uniform appearance. Avoid pulling the knots too tight or leaving them too loose.

Step 9: Complete the Bracelet

Continue knotting according to the alpha pattern chart until you have created the desired message or initials. Once complete, continue knotting the base threads with the background color to complete the rest of the bracelet.

Step 10: Finish the Bracelet

Tie a knot at the end of the bracelet to secure the threads. Trim any excess thread, leaving a small tail.

By following an alpha pattern chart, you can create personalized friendship bracelets with names, messages, or initials. Take your time, refer to the chart carefully, and enjoy the process of bringing your personalized design to life.

4.3 Tips for designing and customizing your own alpha patterns.

Designing and customizing your own alpha patterns for friendship bracelets allows you to create unique and personalized designs. Here are some tips to help you with the process:

1. Plan Your Design: Before starting the pattern, sketch out your desired design on graph paper or use digital design tools. Consider the size and width of your bracelet, as well as the number of threads you'll be using.

2. Keep it Simple: Especially if you're new to designing alpha patterns, start with simple and straightforward designs. As you gain more experience, you can experiment with more intricate and complex patterns.

3. Use Graph Paper: Graph paper provides a helpful grid structure for designing your alpha pattern. Each square on the graph paper can represent a knot in your bracelet. This will help you keep your design organized and easily translatable to the actual bracelet.

4. Experiment with Fonts and Styles: Play around with different fonts and lettering styles to create a unique look for your alpha patterns. Explore different shapes and angles for letters, and try different thicknesses or outlines.

5. Consider Contrast: Ensure good contrast between the background color and the thread color used for the letters or initials. This will make your design more readable and visually appealing.

6. Test Your Design: Before committing to your final pattern, create a small sample using scrap threads to see how your design looks when woven. This will help you identify any issues or adjustments you may need to make.

7. Incorporate Symbols and Icons: Besides letters and initials, consider adding symbols or icons that are meaningful to you or the recipient of the bracelet. This can add a personalized touch and enhance the overall design.

8. Seek Inspiration: Look for inspiration in various sources such as books, websites, or even nature and art. Explore different patterns, color combinations, and techniques that can inspire your own designs.

9. Use Online Pattern Generators: There are online tools and pattern generators specifically designed for creating alpha patterns. These tools can help you visualize and generate patterns based on your desired text and style.

10. Practice and Iterate: Designing alpha patterns is a skill that improves with practice. Don't be afraid to experiment, make mistakes, and iterate on your designs. Each attempt will help you develop your own unique style and improve your pattern-making abilities.

CHAPTER FIVE

BEADED BRACELET

5.1 Techniques for incorporating beads into friendship bracelets, adding texture and visual interest.

Incorporating beads into friendship bracelets can add texture, sparkle, and visual interest to your designs. Here are some techniques you can use to incorporate beads into your friendship bracelets:

1. Single Bead Technique: One simple way to add beads to your bracelet is by using a single bead technique. Here's how:

- Start by creating a few knots using the thread color you want as the background for the bead.

- Slide a bead onto one of the working threads and push it up close to the knots.

- Create a knot on either side of the bead to secure it in place.

- Continue knotting with the background color on either side of the bead to maintain the pattern of your bracelet.

2. Beaded Borders: Another technique is to create beaded borders along the edges of your friendship bracelet. This adds a decorative touch to the design. Here's how:

- Start your bracelet with a few knots of the background color.

- Slide a bead onto one of the working threads and push it up close to the knots.

- Create a knot with the bead right next to the previous knot, securing it in place.

- Repeat this process, alternating between knots with beads and knots without beads along the edge of the bracelet.

3. Beaded Patterns: You can also incorporate beads into the pattern of your friendship bracelet, creating a more intricate design. Here's how:

- Plan your pattern, keeping in mind where you want to place the beads.

- When you reach a point in the pattern where you want to add a bead, slide the bead onto one of the working threads.

- Create a knot with the bead, securing it in place.

- Continue following the pattern, incorporating more beads as desired.

4. Mixed Bead and Knot Technique: For a more varied and textured look, you can alternate between knots and beads in your bracelet. Here's how:

- Begin by creating a few knots with the background color.

- Slide a bead onto one of the working threads and push it up close to the knots.

- Create a knot right next to the bead, securing it in place.

- Continue this pattern, alternating between knots and beads along the length of the bracelet.

5. Random Bead Placement: If you prefer a more random and eclectic look, you can scatter beads throughout your bracelet without following a specific pattern. Simply slide beads onto the working threads at various points, and secure them in place with knots.

Remember to choose beads that have holes large enough to accommodate your threads, and ensure they are compatible with the thickness of your bracelet. Experiment with different bead sizes, shapes, and colors to create unique and eye-catching designs. Beading adds dimension and interest to your friendship bracelets, making them even more special and personalized.

5.2 Step-by-step instructions for creating a beaded bracelet with different bead placement options.

Creating a beaded bracelet with different bead placement options allows you to explore various designs and patterns. Here are step-by-step instructions to guide you through the process:

Materials:

- Friendship bracelet threads

- Beads of your choice

- Scissors

- Clipboard or tape (optional, for securing the bracelet)

Step 1: Prepare the Base Threads

Cut your friendship bracelet threads to the desired length, typically around 60-70 inches (150-180 cm). The number of threads depends on the width you want for your bracelet. Tie a knot at one end of the threads, leaving a small loop.

Step 2: Decide on Bead Placement Options

Choose the bead placement option you want to create for your bracelet. You can consider the following options:

- **Single Bead Technique:** Place beads individually at specific intervals along the bracelet.

- **Beaded Borders:** Create beaded borders by adding beads only along the edges of the bracelet.

- **Beaded Patterns:** Incorporate beads into specific patterns or motifs within the bracelet.

- **Mixed Bead and Knot Technique:** Alternate between knots and beads along the bracelet for a varied look.

- **Random Bead Placement:** Scatter beads randomly throughout the bracelet for an eclectic design.

Step 3: Start Knotting

Begin knotting the base threads with your desired background color. This will serve as the foundation for your bracelet.

Step 4: Add Beads

Follow your chosen bead placement option to incorporate beads into your bracelet. Here's how to do it for each option:

- Single Bead Technique:

- Slide a bead onto one of the working threads.

- Push the bead up close to the knots.

- Create a knot on either side of the bead to secure it in place.

- Continue knotting with the background color on either side of the bead to maintain the pattern of your bracelet.

- Repeat these steps to add more beads at desired intervals.

- Beaded Borders:

- Slide a bead onto one of the working threads.

- Push the bead up close to the knots.

- Create a knot right next to the bead, securing it in place.

- Repeat these steps along the edges of the bracelet to create beaded borders.

- Beaded Patterns:

- Plan your pattern and determine where you want to place the beads.

- Slide a bead onto one of the working threads.

- Push the bead up close to the knots.

- Create a knot right next to the bead, securing it in place.

- Continue following the pattern, incorporating more beads as desired.

- Mixed Bead and Knot Technique:

- Begin by creating a few knots with the background color.

- Slide a bead onto one of the working threads.

- Push the bead up close to the knots.

- Create a knot right next to the bead, securing it in place.

- Continue this pattern, alternating between knots and beads along the length of the bracelet.

- Random Bead Placement:

- Slide beads randomly onto the working threads at various points along the bracelet.

- Create knots on either side of the beads to secure them in place.

Step 5: Complete the Bracelet

Continue knotting and adding beads according to your chosen bead placement option until you reach the desired length for your bracelet. Once you're satisfied with the design, tie a knot at the end of the bracelet to secure the threads. Trim any excess thread, leaving a small tail.

Step 6: Finishing Touches

To ensure the bracelet stays in place while wearing, you can add a closure such as a braided loop and knot or a jewelry clasp. Alternatively, you can tie the ends of the bracelet together to form a simple knot.

By following these steps, you can create a beaded Bracelet.

5.3 Tips for selecting beads, determining their placement, and securing them within the bracelet.

When selecting beads for your friendship bracelet and determining their placement, as well as securing them within the bracelet, consider the following tips:

1. Bead Size and Hole Diameter: Choose beads that are appropriate for the size of your bracelet and have holes large enough to accommodate your threads. Smaller beads work well for delicate and intricate designs, while larger beads can add a bold statement.

2. Bead Material: Consider the material of the beads, such as glass, plastic, wood, or metal, based on the look and feel you want to achieve. Keep in mind that some materials may be more durable or lightweight than others.

3. Color and Texture: Select beads in colors that complement your thread color and overall design. Experiment with different combinations to create contrast, harmony, or a specific color scheme. Additionally, consider beads with interesting textures, finishes, or patterns to add depth and visual interest to your bracelet.

4. Placement and Pattern: Plan the placement of your beads before starting the bracelet. Visualize or sketch out the design to determine where you want to incorporate the beads. Consider patterns, motifs, or symmetrical arrangements to create a cohesive and balanced look.

5. Securing Beads: To keep the beads in place and prevent them from sliding around, create knots on either side of each bead. This will anchor the bead in its intended position within the bracelet.

Ensure the knots are tight enough to secure the bead but not too tight that they distort the shape of the bead or the overall bracelet.

6. Test Placement: Before committing to a particular bead placement, test it out on a small section of the bracelet. This allows you to visualize how the beads will look and make any necessary adjustments or changes before incorporating them into the entire bracelet.

7. Use Bead Caps or Spacer Beads: If you want to add a professional touch or enhance the appearance of the beads, consider using bead caps or spacer beads. These can be placed on either side of a bead to frame it, provide separation between beads, or create a more polished look.

8. Consider Bead Patterns: If you're incorporating multiple beads of different colors or sizes, experiment with creating patterns or gradients within the bracelet. This can add complexity and visual appeal to the design.

9. Be Mindful of Comfort: When placing beads within the bracelet, ensure they won't cause any discomfort or irritation when worn. Be mindful of bead placement near the skin or areas that may rub against clothing or other surfaces.

10. Secure Thread Ends: To prevent the threads from unraveling or the beads from shifting, secure the thread ends at the beginning and end of your bracelet with knots. You can also use adhesive or clear nail polish on the knot to provide additional security.

Remember, bead selection and placement offer endless possibilities for creativity and personalization in your friendship bracelets. Have fun experimenting with different bead combinations, patterns, and techniques to create unique and stunning designs.

CHAPTER SIX

MACRAMÉ BRACELET

6.1 Introduction to macramé techniques, which use knots and braids to create intricate patterns.

Macramé is a versatile and ancient textile art form that utilizes various knots and braids to create intricate patterns and designs. It involves knotting and braiding cords or threads to create decorative and functional pieces. Here is an introduction to some popular macramé techniques:

1. Square Knot: The square knot is one of the fundamental knots in macramé. It is created by crossing the left cord over the middle cords and passing the right cord over the left cord and under the middle cords, creating a square shape. This knot can be repeated in a series to create a flat or diagonal pattern.

2. Half Square Knot: The half square knot is similar to the square knot but involves only one side of the knot. It is created by crossing the left cord over the middle cords and passing the right cord under the left cord and over the middle cords. This creates a half knot, and repeating it in a series creates a twisted or spiral pattern.

3. Double Half Hitch: The double half hitch is a knot used to create diagonal or angled patterns. It is made by wrapping the working cord around the base cord and then passing it through the loop created. This knot is repeated to create a series of diagonal or angled lines.

4. Lark's Head Knot: The lark's head knot is used to attach cords or materials to a base cord or ring. It is created by folding a cord in half, placing the folded end over the base cord, and passing the loose ends through the loop created. This creates a secure attachment point for adding additional cords or materials.

5. Spiral Knot: The spiral knot is a decorative knot used to create spiral patterns. It involves creating multiple half square knots in a circular or spiral motion. This knot is often used to create intricate and eye-catching designs in macramé.

6. Alternating Square Knots: Alternating square knots are used to create patterns with alternating diagonal lines or chevron designs. It involves creating a series of square knots, alternating between the left and right starting cord to create a zigzag or chevron pattern.

7. Fringe and Tassel Techniques: Macramé can also incorporate fringe and tassel techniques to add decorative elements to your designs. Fringe is created by leaving extra lengths of cord at the end of a project and trimming them to desired lengths. Tassels can be made by wrapping cord around a rigid object and tying it off at one end, then cutting the loops at the other end to create a tassel shape.

These are just a few of the many macramé techniques available. As you delve further into the art of macramé, you'll discover more intricate knots and braids that can be combined to create stunning patterns and designs. Macramé offers endless possibilities for creativity and allows you to create beautiful and unique pieces of art, home décor, jewelry, and more.

6.2 Instructions for weaving a macramé friendship bracelet with alternating square knots.

Creating a macramé friendship bracelet using alternating square knots is a fun and customizable project. Here are step-by-step instructions to guide you through the process:

Materials:

- Macramé cord or embroidery floss in your chosen colors

- Scissors

- Clipboard or tape (optional, for securing the bracelet)

Step 1: Prepare the Base Cords

Cut two equal lengths of macramé cord or embroidery floss, each measuring approximately 60-70 inches (150-180 cm) long. These will serve as your base cords.

Fold them in half and align the ends, creating a loop at the folded end. This loop will be used to secure the bracelet later.

Step 2: Attach the Working Cord

Cut a shorter piece of cord or floss, approximately 12-18 inches (30-45 cm) long. This will be your working cord. Fold it in half and place the folded end underneath the base cords, with the loop facing upward. Take the loose ends of the working cord and pass them through the loop, creating a lark's head knot. Pull the loose ends to tighten the working cord securely onto the base cords.

Step 3: Start the Alternating Square Knots

Now that your working cord is attached, you can begin creating the alternating square knots. Here's how to do it:

- **Step 1:** Separate the base cords into four strands. You will have two outer strands (left and right) and two middle strands.

- **Step 2:** Take the left outer strand and cross it over the middle strands, forming a loop on the left side.

- **Step 3:** Take the right outer strand and pass it over the left strand and under the middle strands, coming up through the loop on the right side.

- **Step 4:** Pull the left and right strands tightly to create the first half of the square knot.

- **Step 5:** Repeat the process, but this time start with the right outer strand. Cross it over the middle strands to the right side, then take the left outer strand and pass it over the right strand and under the middle strands, coming up through the loop on the left side.

- **Step 6:** Pull the left and right strands tightly to complete the square knot.

Step 4: Repeat the Alternating Square Knots

Continue repeating the steps above to create a series of alternating square knots. As you progress, the knots will start forming a pattern. Make sure to pull the knots tightly each time to create a neat and secure bracelet.

Step 5: Adjust the Length

Continue knotting until your bracelet reaches the desired length. Keep in mind that the bracelet will slightly shorten when worn, so it's better to make it a bit longer. You can periodically try the bracelet on to check the fit.

Step 6: Finish the Bracelet

To finish the bracelet, you have a few options:

- **Option 1:** Tie a knot at the end of the last square knot, leaving a small tail. Trim any excess cord or floss.

- **Option 2:** Create a braided or twisted ending by dividing the remaining cords into two sections and twisting or braiding them together. Tie a knot at the end to secure it, and trim any excess cord or floss.

Step 7: Secure the Bracelet (Optional)

If desired, you can secure the bracelet to a clipboard or tape it down to a surface to keep it taut while working. This will make the knotting process easier and prevent the bracelet from shifting.

Once you've finished the bracelet and secured the ends, you can proudly wear or gift your macramé friendship bracelet with alternating square knots. Experiment with different cord colors, bead accents, or additional decorative elements to personalize your designs and create unique variations

6.3 Tips for experimenting with different knot combinations and incorporating beads or charms.

When it comes to experimenting with different knot combinations and incorporating beads or charms into your macramé projects, here are some helpful tips:

1. Start with Basic Knots: Begin by mastering the fundamental macramé knots, such as square knots, half square knots, and double half hitches. These knots serve as the building blocks for more intricate patterns and designs.

2. Mix Knots and Patterns: Combine different knot variations and patterns to create unique textures and visual interest in your macramé piece. Experiment with alternating square knots, diagonal knots, twisted knots, or even knotting in different directions.

3. Play with Color: Macramé allows for endless possibilities when it comes to color combinations. Incorporate multiple colors of cords or threads to create striped or gradient effects. Consider using contrasting colors for a bold statement or complementary colors for a harmonious look.

4. Integrate Beads or Charms: Beads or charms can add a delightful touch to your macramé projects. Here are a few ways to incorporate them:

- Use beads as spacer elements between knots or as focal points within a pattern.

- Thread beads onto individual cords before knotting to create a beaded accent.

- Attach charms or pendants to the finished macramé piece using jump rings or by incorporating them into the knotting itself.

5. Be Mindful of Bead Placement: When adding beads to your macramé, consider their size, weight, and position within the pattern. Ensure that the knots are tight enough to hold the beads securely in place without sliding or shifting.

6. Experiment with Bead Patterns: Create patterns or motifs with beads by incorporating them in specific sequences or arrangements. Try using beads of different sizes, colors, or shapes to create eye-catching designs within your macramé piece.

7. Consider Different Types of Beads: Explore various bead materials, such as glass, wood, metal, or acrylic, to achieve different looks and textures. Each type of bead will add its own unique character to the macramé design.

8. Plan and Sketch: Before starting a project that incorporates beads or charms, plan out your design and sketch it on paper. This will help you visualize the placement of knots, beads, and any other elements you want to include.

9. Practice and Experiment: Don't be afraid to try new knot combinations, bead placements, or charm arrangements. Macramé is a versatile art form, and the more you practice and experiment, the more you'll discover your own unique style and techniques.

Remember, the beauty of macramé lies in its versatility and the freedom to explore your creativity. Have fun with your projects, and don't be afraid to take risks and try new ideas. With time and practice, you'll develop your own personal style and create stunning macramé pieces that reflect your unique vision.

CHAPTER SEVEN

DOUBLE CHAIN BRACELET

7.1 Detailed guide for creating a double chain friendship bracelet using the double chain stitch.

Creating a double chain friendship bracelet using the double chain stitch is a fun and visually appealing project. Here is a step-by-step guide to help you create this bracelet:

Materials:

- Embroidery floss or thin cord in your chosen colors

- Scissors

- Clipboard or tape (optional, for securing the bracelet)

Step 1: Prepare the Base Cords

Cut three equal lengths of embroidery floss or thin cord, each measuring approximately 30 inches (75 cm) long. These will serve as your base cords. Align the ends and tie a knot at one end, leaving a small loop.

Step 2: Start the Double Chain Stitch

- **Step 1:** Separate the base cords into two groups, with two cords in one group and one cord in the other.

- **Step 2:** Take the right cord from the group of two and cross it over the middle of the other two cords, forming a loop on the right side.

- **Step 3:** Take the left cord from the group of two and pass it over the right cord and under the two middle cords, coming up through the loop on the left side.

- **Step 4:** Pull both ends of the left cord to tighten the stitch, creating a chain-like appearance.

- **Step 5:** Repeat the double chain stitch with the same group of cords, starting with the right cord crossing over the middle cords and the left cord passing over and under, coming up through the loop on the left side.

- **Step 6:** Continue repeating the double chain stitch with the same group of cords until you achieve the desired length.

Step 3: Adding the Third Cord

- **Step 1:** After completing a row of double chain stitches with the two-cord group, it's time to introduce the third cord into the pattern.

- **Step 2:** Take the right cord from the group of two and place it in the middle, between the two middle cords.

- **Step 3:** Take the left cord from the group of two and place it on the right side, crossing it over the right cord and under the two middle cords.

- **Step 4:** Continue with the double chain stitch, starting with the right cord crossing over the middle cords and the left cord passing over and under, coming up through the loop on the left side.

Step 4: Repeat the Double Chain Stitch with Three Cords

- **Step 1:** Now that the third cord is introduced, repeat the double chain stitch with all three cords.

- **Step 2:** Take the right cord, cross it over the middle cords, and create a loop on the right side.

- **Step 3:** Take the left cord, pass it over the right cord and under the middle cords, coming up through the loop on the left side.

- Step 4: Pull both ends of the left cord to tighten the stitch.

- Step 5: Repeat the double chain stitch with all three cords until you reach the desired length.

Step 5: Finishing the Bracelet

- Step 1: Once you've reached the desired length, tie a knot at the end of the last double chain stitch, leaving a small tail.

- Step 2: Trim any excess cord or floss.

Step 6: Secure the Bracelet (Optional)

If desired, you can secure the bracelet to a clipboard or tape it down to a surface to keep it taut while working. This will make the stitching process easier and prevent the bracelet from shifting.

By following these steps, you can create a beautiful double chain friendship bracelet using the double chain stitch. Experiment with different color combinations and enjoy the process of weaving a unique piece of handmade jewelry.

7.2 Instructions for adding color variations and patterns within the double chain design.

To add color variations and patterns within the double chain design of your friendship bracelet, you can incorporate different techniques and strategies. Here are some instructions to help you achieve that:

1. Two-Tone Color Scheme:

- Choose two different colors of embroidery floss or thin cord for your base cords.

- Divide your base cords into two groups, with one color in each group.

- Alternate the groups of cords as you perform the double chain stitch. For example, use the first group for one stitch, then switch to the second group for the next stitch, and continue alternating throughout the bracelet.

2. Striped Pattern:

- Select multiple colors of embroidery floss or thin cord for your base cords.

- Divide your base cords into multiple groups, each representing a different color.

- Create stripes by working a certain number of stitches with one group of cords, then switching to the next group to continue the pattern. For example, work five stitches with the first group, then switch to the second group and work five stitches, and so on.

3. Ombre Effect:

- Choose a gradient of colors that transition from one shade to another. This can be achieved by selecting multiple shades of the same color or choosing different colors that blend well together.

- Start with one color for the initial stitches, then gradually introduce the next color in the gradient, working more stitches with the new color as you progress. This will create a smooth transition and give your bracelet an ombre effect.

4. Checkerboard Pattern:

- Select two contrasting colors for your base cords.

- Work the double chain stitch with the first color for a set number of stitches (e.g., four stitches).

- Switch to the second color and work the same number of stitches.

- Repeat this pattern of alternating colors for the desired length of the bracelet.

5. Introducing Additional Colors:

- If you want to incorporate more colors within the double chain design, you can use additional cords to create accents or small sections of contrasting colors.

- For example, when working with three base cords, you can introduce a fourth cord of a different color and incorporate it into the double chain stitch periodically. This will create a pop of color within the design.

Remember to plan your color variations and patterns in advance to achieve the desired effect. Consider sketching out your design or creating a color chart to visualize how the colors will interact and transition within the bracelet.

By incorporating these techniques, you can add color variations and patterns to your double chain friendship bracelet, making it more visually interesting and unique. Feel free to experiment with different color combinations and patterns to create a bracelet that reflects your personal style and creativity.

7.3 Tips for achieving symmetry and a smooth finish.

Achieving symmetry and a smooth finish in your friendship bracelets can enhance their overall appearance. Here are some tips to help you achieve that:

1. **Consistent Tension:** Maintain a consistent tension while working on your bracelet. Keep the cords or floss taut but

not overly tight. Consistent tension will help ensure that the knots and stitches are evenly spaced and uniform throughout the bracelet.

2. Measure and Cut Cords/Floss Evenly: Use a ruler or measuring tape to ensure that your base cords or floss strands are cut to the same length. This will help maintain symmetry and prevent one side of the bracelet from being longer than the other.

3. Use Tape or a Clipboard: Securing your bracelet to a clipboard or taping it down to a surface can help keep it taut and prevent it from shifting or distorting while you work. This will contribute to a more even and symmetrical result.

4. Count Stitches and Rows: Keep track of the number of stitches or rows you are working on each side of the bracelet. This will help you maintain symmetry and ensure that both sides match in terms of pattern, length, and design.

5. Regularly Check for Symmetry: Frequently compare both sides of your bracelet to ensure they mirror each other. Check the pattern, stitch count, and any color variations to make adjustments if needed.

6. Take Breaks: It's a good idea to take regular breaks while working on your bracelet. Stepping away for a moment and then coming back to it with fresh eyes can help you notice any imbalances or inconsistencies that may have been overlooked while working continuously.

7. Practice and Patience: Achieving symmetry and a smooth finish may take practice. Be patient with yourself and keep practicing your knotting techniques. With time, you'll develop more control and consistency in your work.

8. Finishing Techniques: Pay attention to the finishing techniques you use to complete your bracelet. Whether you're using knots, clasps, or other closures, ensure they are secure and balanced to maintain the overall symmetry and provide a polished finish.

9. Trim Excess Material: Once your bracelet is complete, trim any excess cords or floss carefully. Use sharp scissors to achieve clean cuts and maintain a neat appearance.

10. Practice Quality Control: Before gifting or wearing your bracelet, perform a thorough quality check. Look for any loose or uneven stitches, adjust them if necessary, and make sure the overall finish is smooth and symmetrical.

Remember, achieving symmetry and a smooth finish comes with practice and attention to detail. Take your time, be mindful of your techniques, and don't be afraid to make adjustments as needed. With practice, your friendship bracelets will become more symmetrical and beautifully finished.

CHAPTER EIGHT

HEART PATTERN BRACELET

8.1 Instructions for weaving a friendship bracelet with a heart-shaped pattern using the forward knot technique.

Creating a friendship bracelet with a heart-shaped pattern using the forward knot technique can be a delightful project. Here's a step-by-step guide to help you weave the bracelet:

Materials:

- Embroidery floss or thin cord in your desired colors

- Scissors

- Clipboard or tape (optional, for securing the bracelet)

Step 1: Prepare the Base Cords

1. Cut three equal lengths of embroidery floss or thin cord, each measuring approximately 30 inches (75 cm) long. These will serve as your base cords.

2. Align the ends of the cords and tie a knot at one end, leaving a small loop. This loop will be used to secure the bracelet during the weaving process.

Step 2: Start the Bracelet

1. Take the leftmost cord and position it over the other two cords, forming a backward "L" shape.

2. Take the rightmost cord and position it under the leftmost cord, creating a loop on the right side.

3. Pass the rightmost cord through the loop from underneath, pulling it upwards to create a knot.

4. Tighten the knot by pulling both ends of the rightmost cord gently.

Step 3: Create the Heart Pattern

1. Repeat Step 2 to create a row of forward knots using the rightmost cord as the working cord.

2. At the end of the row, switch to the leftmost cord as the working cord.

3. Create a row of forward knots using the leftmost cord.

4. Repeat this alternating pattern of rows, using the rightmost cord and then the leftmost cord as the working cord, to form the heart shape.

5. As you progress, you'll notice the heart shape forming. Ensure the knots are tight and secure to maintain the shape.

Step 4: Continue Weaving

1. Repeat the alternating pattern of rows until you reach the desired length for your bracelet.

2. If you want a solid heart pattern, continue weaving the heart shape for the entire length of the bracelet.

3. If you prefer a more open design, you can add additional rows of forward knots between the heart pattern.

Step 5: Finishing the Bracelet

1. Once you've reached the desired length, tie a knot at the end of the last row to secure the weaving.

2. Trim any excess cord or floss, leaving a small tail.

3. You can add clasps, braided ends, or additional knots to finish the bracelet, depending on your preference.

Step 6: Secure the Bracelet (Optional)

If desired, you can secure the bracelet to a clipboard or tape it down to a surface to keep it taut while working. This will make the weaving process easier and prevent the bracelet from shifting.

By following these steps, you can create a lovely friendship bracelet with a heart-shaped pattern using the forward knot technique. Experiment with different colors and enjoy the process of weaving a heartfelt gift for your friend or loved one.

8.2 Tips for positioning and shaping the heart design for optimal visual impact.

To position and shape the heart design in your friendship bracelet for optimal visual impact, consider the following tips:

1. Bracelet Placement: Decide where you want the heart design to be positioned on the bracelet. You can choose to have a centered heart or place it closer to one end. Consider how the pattern will appear when the bracelet is worn.

2. Adjust Knot Tension: Pay attention to the tension of your knots as you weave the heart design. Ensure that the knots are tight enough to maintain the shape but not so tight that they distort the design. Consistent tension throughout the weaving process will help create a well-defined heart shape.

3. Use Contrast Colors: Select contrasting colors for the heart pattern to make it stand out. For example, choose a bright color for the heart and a neutral color for the background. This will enhance the visibility of the heart and make it more visually striking.

4. Experiment with Size and Proportions: Consider the size of your bracelet and the desired size of the heart pattern. Larger bracelets can accommodate larger heart designs, while smaller bracelets may require smaller and more compact hearts. Experiment with different sizes and proportions to find what works best for your bracelet.

5. Shape Definition: Pay attention to the shaping of the heart by adjusting the angle and placement of each row. The point of the heart should be well-defined and the curves smooth. Take your time while weaving and adjust the tension and placement of knots as needed to achieve the desired shape.

6. Plan Ahead: Before starting the heart pattern, sketch or visualize how you want the final design to appear. This will help you determine the number of rows needed for each side of the heart and ensure symmetry and balance.

7. Step Back and Assess: Regularly step back and take a look at your progress to evaluate the shape and positioning of the heart. This will allow you to make adjustments if needed and ensure the optimal visual impact of the design.

8. Practice: Creating the perfect heart shape may require practice and experimentation. Don't be discouraged if your first attempts don't turn out exactly as planned. With practice, you'll develop a better sense of shaping and positioning the heart design.

Remember, each friendship bracelet is unique, and your personal touch and creativity will make it special. By following these tips and allowing yourself to explore different techniques, you'll be able to position and shape the heart design in your friendship bracelet to achieve maximum visual impact.

8.3 Variations and ideas for incorporating different color combinations or adding accents.

Incorporating different color combinations and accents in your friendship bracelets can add depth and visual interest to your designs. Here are some variations and ideas to consider:

1. Gradient or Ombre Effect: Choose a color palette that transitions from one shade to another, creating a gradient or ombre effect in your bracelet. Start with one color and gradually transition to another by using progressively lighter or darker shades of the same color. This adds a beautiful visual element to your bracelet.

2. Color Blocking: Create bold and distinct sections of color by using contrasting colors in your bracelet. Alternate blocks of different colors to create a vibrant and eye-catching design. This works well with geometric patterns or simple knotting techniques.

3. Two-Tone or Three-Tone Bracelets: Instead of using a single color for the entire bracelet, consider using two or three complementary colors. You can create alternating rows or sections of different colors, resulting in a dynamic and colorful bracelet.

4. Accents with Metallic Thread: Introduce a touch of shimmer and sparkle to your friendship bracelet by incorporating metallic thread. Use it as an accent color alongside regular embroidery floss or as a separate strand to create a focal point or highlight specific elements of your design.

5. Beads and Charms: Enhance your friendship bracelets by adding beads or charms. You can intersperse beads throughout the bracelet, create patterns with them, or use them as focal points. Consider beads in coordinating or contrasting colors to complement your chosen color scheme.

6. Embroidery Stitches: Explore the use of embroidery stitches in your friendship bracelets to add texture and dimension. Incorporate stitches like French knots, satin stitches, or cross stitches to create intricate patterns or accent specific areas of your bracelet.

7. Natural Elements: Incorporate natural elements like shells, small stones, or wooden beads into your friendship bracelet. These additions can add an organic and unique touch to your design, connecting it to nature.

8. Personalization with Initials or Symbols: Use alphabet beads or create your own letter patterns to incorporate initials or meaningful symbols into your friendship bracelet. This adds a personalized touch and can be a great gift idea for a friend.

9. Play with Patterns: Experiment with various knotting patterns such as chevrons, zigzags, diamonds, or waves. Combine different patterns or create your own to make your bracelets truly unique.

10. Mix and Match: Don't be afraid to combine different ideas and techniques. Mix color variations, bead accents, and patterned sections to create one-of-a-kind friendship bracelets that reflect your personal style and creativity.

Remember, the possibilities are endless when it comes to color combinations and accents in friendship bracelet making. Let your imagination guide you and have fun exploring different variations and ideas.

CHAPTER NINE

WRAPAROUND BRACELET

9.1 Step-by-step instructions for creating a wraparound friendship bracelet that can be worn as a multi-layered accessory.

Creating a wraparound friendship bracelet that can be worn as a multi-layered accessory is a fun project. Here's a step-by-step guide to help you create one:

Materials:

- Embroidery floss or thin cord in your desired colors

- Scissors

- Clipboard or tape (optional, for securing the bracelet)

Step 1: Prepare the Base Cords

1. Cut several equal lengths of embroidery floss or thin cord, each measuring approximately 30 inches (75 cm) long. The number of cords you cut will depend on how many layers you want in your wraparound bracelet.

2. Align the ends of the cords and tie a knot at one end, leaving a small loop. This loop will be used to secure the bracelet during the weaving process.

Step 2: Start the Bracelet

1. Take all the cords together and tie a knot near the looped end, leaving a small tail. This will serve as the starting point for your bracelet.

2. Secure the bracelet to a clipboard or tape it down to a surface to keep it taut while working. This will make the

weaving process easier and prevent the bracelet from shifting.

Step 3: Weave the Bracelet

1. Separate the cords into two equal groups. For example, if you have eight cords, divide them into two groups of four.

2. Choose one group of cords to work with first. Take the rightmost cord and position it over the other cords, forming a backward "L" shape.

3. Take the leftmost cord from the same group and position it under the rightmost cord, creating a loop on the left side.

4. Pass the leftmost cord through the loop from underneath, pulling it upwards to

create a knot. Tighten the knot by pulling both ends of the leftmost cord gently.

5. Repeat steps 2-4 with the same group of cords to create a row of knots.

6. Switch to the other group of cords and repeat steps 2-5 to create another row of knots.

7. Continue alternating between the two groups of cords, creating rows of knots, until your bracelet reaches the desired length.

Step 4: Finishing the Bracelet

1. Once you've reached the desired length, tie a knot at the end of the last row to secure the weaving.

2. Trim any excess cord or floss, leaving a small tail.

3. You can add clasps, braided ends, or additional knots to finish the bracelet, depending on your preference.

Step 5: Layering the Bracelet

1. Wrap the bracelet around your wrist, starting with the end where you tied the initial knot.

2. Continue wrapping the bracelet around your wrist, overlapping the layers until you reach the desired layered effect.

3. Adjust the tightness of the layers to ensure a comfortable fit.

4. Secure the bracelet by tying the ends together or using a small clasp or button closure.

By following these steps, you can create a wraparound friendship bracelet that can be worn as a multi-layered accessory. Experiment with different color combinations, knotting patterns, and layering techniques to create unique and personalized bracelets that reflect your style. Enjoy the process and have fun creating a stylish accessory to wear or gift to a friend.

9.2 Tips for selecting the right length of thread and ensuring a comfortable fit.

When creating a wraparound friendship bracelet, selecting the right length of thread and ensuring a comfortable fit are essential. Here are some tips to help you with these aspects:

1. Measure your wrist: Use a flexible measuring tape or a piece of string to measure your wrist's circumference. Add a small amount of extra length for a comfortable fit and room for the bracelet to wrap around multiple times.

2. Consider the layers: Determine how many layers you want in your wraparound bracelet. Each layer will require additional length, so factor this into your measurement. For example, if you want three layers and your wrist measures 6 inches, you'll need at least 18 inches of thread per layer.

3. Add extra length: It's always better to have slightly more thread than you think you'll need. Adding a few extra inches to your measurement ensures you have enough thread to work with and reduces the risk of running out before completing your bracelet.

4. Test it out: Before starting your bracelet, cut a piece of thread to your measured length and wrap it around your wrist multiple times. Check if it feels comfortable and allows for easy movement. If it's too tight or too loose, adjust the length accordingly.

5. Account for knots and finishing: Remember to consider the extra length needed for tying knots, securing the bracelet, and any additional finishing details. These can add a few inches to the overall length requirement.

6. Practice with a mock-up: If you're unsure about the length, try creating a mock-up bracelet with inexpensive materials or scrap thread. This will give you a better idea of how the final bracelet will fit and allow you to make any necessary adjustments.

7. Adjustability options: If you want more flexibility in sizing, consider adding an adjustable closure to your bracelet, such as a sliding knot or an extension chain. This allows the wearer to adjust the fit as needed.

8. Comfort is key: Ensure that the bracelet is not too tight, as it may restrict blood flow or cause discomfort. On the other hand, if it's too loose, it may slip off easily. Aim for a snug but comfortable fit that allows for movement and flexibility.

Remember, everyone's wrist size and comfort preferences may vary, so it's essential to consider these factors when determining the length of thread for your wraparound friendship bracelet. By following these tips and taking the time to measure and test, you can create a bracelet that fits well and is enjoyable to wear.

9.3 Ideas for personalizing wraparound bracelets with unique closures or charms.

Personalizing wraparound bracelets with unique closures or charms can add a special touch and make them even more meaningful. Here are some ideas to inspire you:

1. Button Closure: Attach a decorative button to one end of the bracelet and create a loop on the opposite end to secure the button. Choose a button that complements the style of your bracelet or has personal significance to you.

2. Lobster Clasp: Use a lobster clasp as a closure for your bracelet. Attach one end of the bracelet to the clasp using a jump ring or by directly knotting the threads around it. This allows for easy fastening and removal of the bracelet.

3. Sliding Knot: Create an adjustable closure by using a sliding knot. Leave long tails at the ends of your bracelet and tie sliding knots to secure them. This allows the wearer to adjust the fit by sliding the knots up or down.

4. Beaded Toggle Clasp: Incorporate a beaded toggle clasp into your bracelet design. Create a beaded loop on one end and attach a decorative toggle bar to the other end. This adds a unique and eye-catching closure.

5. Magnetic Closure: Use a magnetic clasp as a convenient closure option. Attach one end of the bracelet to each side of the magnetic clasp, ensuring a secure fit. This type of closure is easy to use and adds a modern touch.

6. Birthstone Charms: Add birthstone charms to your bracelet to represent your own birth month or the birth months of loved ones. Attach the charms using jump rings or by knotting them onto the threads.

7. Initial Charms: Personalize your bracelet with initial charms that represent your name or the initials of someone special to you. Choose charms that can be easily attached to the bracelet using jump rings.

8. Symbolic Charms: Select charms that hold personal meaning or symbolize something significant to you. It could be a charm that represents a hobby, a favorite animal, a spiritual symbol, or any other meaningful representation.

9. Tassel Closure: Attach a tassel to one end of the bracelet as a decorative and unique closure. You can make your own tassel using embroidery floss or purchase pre-made tassels in various colors and styles.

10. Unique Knotting or Braiding: Experiment with different knotting or braiding techniques to create an interesting and personalized closure. For example, you can create a decorative knot or braid at the ends of the bracelet to serve as a closure.

Remember, the closure or charm you choose should reflect your personal style and add a touch of individuality to your wraparound bracelet. Feel free to mix and match ideas or come up with your own unique closures and charms to make your bracelet truly special.

CHAPTER TEN

ZIGZAG BRACELET

10.1 Introduction to the zigzag pattern, which creates a visually striking bracelet design.

The zigzag pattern is a visually striking design that can add a unique touch to your friendship bracelets. It consists of diagonal lines that form a zigzag pattern, creating an eye-catching and dynamic look. Here's an introduction to creating a zigzag pattern in your friendship bracelets:

Materials:

- Embroidery floss or thin cord in your desired colors

- Scissors

- Clipboard or tape (optional, for securing the bracelet)

Step-by-step instructions:

1. Choose your colors: Select the colors you want to use for your zigzag pattern. You can use two or more colors to create contrast and make the design more prominent.

2. Prepare the base cords: Cut several equal lengths of embroidery floss or thin cord, each measuring approximately 30 inches (75 cm) long. The number of cords you cut will depend on the width and layers of your bracelet.

3. Start the bracelet: Take all the cords together and tie a knot at one end, leaving a small loop. This loop will be used to secure the bracelet during the weaving process.

4. Secure the bracelet: Secure the bracelet to a clipboard or tape it down to a surface to keep it taut while working. This will make the weaving process easier and prevent the bracelet from shifting.

5. Create the first diagonal line: Separate the cords into two equal groups. For example, if you have eight cords, divide them into two groups of four. Choose one group to work with first.

- Take the rightmost cord from the group and position it diagonally over the cords in the other group.

- Take the leftmost cord from the same group and position it diagonally under the cords in the other group.

- Pass the leftmost cord through the loop formed by the rightmost cord, pulling it upwards to create a knot. Tighten the knot by pulling both ends of the leftmost cord gently.

- Repeat this process with the same group of cords to create a row of diagonal knots.

6. Create the next diagonal line: Switch to the other group of cords and repeat the process to create a row of diagonal knots in the opposite direction. Alternate between the two groups to create the zigzag pattern.

7. Continue weaving: Keep repeating steps 5 and 6, alternating between the groups of cords, until your bracelet reaches the desired length. You can create multiple layers of the zigzag pattern by repeating the process with additional groups of cords.

8. Finish the bracelet: Once you've reached the desired length, tie a knot at the end of the last row to secure the weaving. Trim any excess cord or floss, leaving a small tail. You can add clasps, braided ends, or additional knots to finish the bracelet, depending on your preference.

By following these steps, you can create a visually striking zigzag pattern in your friendship bracelets. Experiment with different color combinations, widths, and layering techniques to create unique and personalized bracelets that stand out. Enjoy the process and have fun weaving beautiful zigzag patterns in your friendship bracelets!

10.2 Instructions for weaving a zigzag friendship bracelet using the forward knot technique.

Sure! Here are step-by-step instructions for weaving a zigzag friendship bracelet using the forward knot technique:

Materials:

- Embroidery floss or thin cord in your desired colors

- Scissors

- Clipboard or tape (optional, for securing the bracelet)

Step-by-step instructions:

1. Choose your colors: Select the colors you want to use for your zigzag pattern. You can use two or more colors to create contrast and make the design more prominent.

2. Prepare the base cords: Cut several equal lengths of embroidery floss or thin cord, each measuring approximately 30 inches (75 cm) long. The number of cords you cut will depend on the width and layers of your bracelet.

3. Start the bracelet: Take all the cords together and tie a knot at one end, leaving a small loop. This loop will be used to secure the bracelet during the weaving process.

4. Secure the bracelet: Secure the bracelet to a clipboard or tape it down to a surface to keep it taut while working. This will make the weaving process easier and prevent the bracelet from shifting.

5. Create the first diagonal line: Separate the cords into two equal groups. For example, if you have eight cords, divide them into two groups of four. Choose one group to work with first.

- Take the rightmost cord from the group and position it diagonally over the cords in the other group.

- Take the leftmost cord from the same group and position it diagonally under the cords in the other group.

- Using the forward knot technique, tie a forward knot with the leftmost cord over the cords in the other group. The leftmost cord should now be on the right side of the group.

- Repeat this process with the same group of cords to create a row of diagonal forward knots.

6. Create the next diagonal line: Switch to the other group of cords and repeat the process to create a row of diagonal forward knots in the opposite direction. Alternate between the two groups to create the zigzag pattern.

7. Continue weaving: Keep repeating steps 5 and 6, alternating between the groups of cords, until your bracelet reaches the desired length. You can create multiple layers of the zigzag pattern by repeating the process with additional groups of cords.

8. Finish the bracelet: Once you've reached the desired length, tie a knot at the end of the last row to secure the weaving. Trim any excess cord or floss, leaving a small tail. You can add clasps, braided ends, or additional knots to finish the bracelet, depending on your preference.

By following these steps and using the forward knot technique, you can create a beautiful zigzag friendship bracelet. Feel free to experiment with different color combinations and patterns to make your bracelet unique and personalized. Have fun weaving!

10.3 Tips for alternating colors and achieving clean lines in the zigzag pattern.

Achieving clean lines and alternating colors effectively in the zigzag pattern can enhance the overall appearance of your friendship bracelet. Here are some tips to help you achieve that:

1. Plan your color sequence: Before starting the bracelet, plan the color sequence for your zigzag pattern. This will ensure a balanced distribution of colors and a visually pleasing result. Consider using contrasting or complementary colors to make the zigzag pattern stand out.

2. Maintain consistent tension: Consistent tension is key to achieving clean lines in your zigzag pattern. Make sure to pull each knot tight enough, but not too tight that it distorts the shape of the bracelet. Consistent tension will keep the knots aligned and the colors neatly separated.

3. Use tape or clips: To keep the cords in place and maintain clean lines, you can use small pieces of tape or clips to secure the cords on the sides. This will prevent them from shifting or getting tangled while you weave, resulting in a more precise zigzag pattern.

4. Be mindful of color placement: Pay attention to the placement of colors as you weave the zigzag pattern. If you want distinct color separation, ensure that the same color cord is consistently positioned over or under the cords of the other color. This will create crisp lines and prevent color bleeding.

5. Trim excess thread or floss: Regularly trim any excess thread or floss after each row of knots. This will help maintain a neat and tidy appearance as you weave the zigzag pattern. It's easier to trim small amounts frequently rather than waiting until the end, which can result in uneven edges.

6. Take breaks to assess your progress: It's a good idea to take breaks occasionally and step back to assess your progress. This will allow you to spot any inconsistencies or areas where the color placement may need adjustment. Making small corrections as you go will help maintain a clean and precise zigzag pattern.

7. Practice and experiment: Like any skill, achieving clean lines and alternating colors in the zigzag pattern takes practice. Don't be discouraged if your first attempts are not perfect. Keep practicing and experimenting with different color combinations and techniques to improve your skills and achieve the desired results.

By following these tips and paying attention to color placement and tension, you can create a beautiful zigzag pattern with clean lines and alternating colors in your friendship bracelet. Enjoy the process and have fun creating stunning designs!

CHAPTER ELEVEN

ADVANCED PATTERN BRACELET

11.1 Challenge yourself with a more intricate friendship bracelet pattern that combines different knotting techniques.

Certainly! Here's a more intricate friendship bracelet pattern that combines different knotting techniques:

Name: "Diamond Burst Bracelet"

Materials:

- Embroidery floss or thin cord in your desired colors

- Scissors

- Clipboard or tape (optional, for securing the bracelet)

Pattern Description:

The Diamond Burst Bracelet features a central diamond-shaped motif surrounded by a burst of diagonal lines. It combines the forward knot technique for the diamond shape and the chevron pattern for the diagonal lines. The result is a visually striking bracelet with an intricate design.

Instructions:

1. Choose your colors: Select the colors you want to use for the bracelet. You'll need at least three colors—one for the diamond shape and two for the diagonal lines. Consider using contrasting colors for the diamond and complementary colors for the diagonal lines.

2. Prepare the base cords: Cut several equal lengths of embroidery floss or thin cord, each measuring approximately 30 inches (75 cm) long. The number of cords you cut will depend on the width and layers of your bracelet.

3. Start the bracelet: Take all the cords together and tie a knot at one end, leaving a small loop. This loop will be used to secure the bracelet during the weaving process.

4. Secure the bracelet: Secure the bracelet to a clipboard or tape it down to a surface to keep it taut while working. This will make the weaving process easier and prevent the bracelet from shifting.

5. Weave the diamond shape:

- Take the center cords (usually two or four cords) and separate them from the rest.

- Using the forward knot technique, create diagonal knots with the center cords, forming a diamond shape. You can reference the instructions for creating a diamond shape bracelet in a previous section.

- Once the diamond shape is complete, return the center cords to the main group.

6. Weave the diagonal lines:

- Separate the cords into two equal groups.

- Take the rightmost cord from one group and position it diagonally over the cords in the other group.

- Take the leftmost cord from the same group and position it diagonally under the cords in the other group.

- Using the chevron pattern (forward knots or backward knots), create a row of diagonal knots.

- Repeat this process with the same group of cords to continue the diagonal lines.

- Switch to the other group of cords and repeat the process to create a row of diagonal knots in the opposite direction.

- Alternate between the two groups to create the burst of diagonal lines around the diamond shape.

7. Continue weaving:

- Keep repeating step 6, alternating between the groups of cords, until your bracelet reaches the desired length.

- You can adjust the number of rows for the diamond shape and the burst of diagonal lines based on your preference.

8. Finish the bracelet:

- Once you've reached the desired length, tie a knot at the end of the last row to secure the weaving.

- Trim any excess cord or floss, leaving a small tail.

- You can add clasps, braided ends, or additional knots to finish the bracelet, depending on your preference.

The Diamond Burst Bracelet pattern combines different knotting techniques to create an intricate design. It's a challenging project that will test your skills and patience. Enjoy the process and the beautiful results of your hard work!

11.2 Step-by-step instructions for weaving a complex pattern, such as a diamond or star design.

Certainly! Here are step-by-step instructions for weaving a complex pattern, specifically a diamond or star design:

Name: "Stellar Diamond Bracelet"

Materials:

- Embroidery floss or thin cord in your desired colors

- Scissors

- Clipboard or tape (optional, for securing the bracelet)

Pattern Description:

The Stellar Diamond Bracelet features a central diamond or star-shaped motif surrounded by intricate patterns. It combines various knotting techniques to create a visually captivating design.

Instructions:

1. Choose your colors: Select the colors you want to use for the bracelet. Consider using contrasting or complementary colors to make the design stand out.

2. Prepare the base cords: Cut several equal lengths of embroidery floss or thin cord, each measuring approximately 30 inches (75 cm) long. The number of cords you cut will depend on the width and layers of your bracelet.

3. Start the bracelet: Take all the cords together and tie a knot at one end, leaving a small loop. This loop will be used to secure the bracelet during the weaving process.

4. Secure the bracelet: Secure the bracelet to a clipboard or tape it down to a surface to keep it taut while working. This will make the weaving process easier and prevent the bracelet from shifting.

5. Weave the central motif:

- Choose whether you want to create a diamond or star-shaped motif for the center.

- If creating a diamond:

- Take the center cords (usually two or four cords) and separate them from the rest.

- Using the forward knot technique, create diagonal knots with the center cords, forming a diamond shape. You can reference the instructions for creating a diamond shape bracelet in a previous section.

- Once the diamond shape is complete, return the center cords to the main group.

- If creating a star:

- Take the center cords (usually five or more cords) and separate them from the rest.

- Using the forward knot technique, create a series of knots that radiate from a central point, forming a star shape. You can reference the instructions for creating a star shape bracelet in a previous section.

- Once the star shape is complete, return the center cords to the main group.

6. Weave the intricate patterns:

- Now that you have the central motif, you can begin weaving the intricate patterns around it.

- Explore different knotting techniques such as forward knots, backward knots, square knots, or combination knots to create various patterns.

- Alternate between different colors and knotting techniques to achieve the desired effect. You can reference the knotting techniques and patterns covered in the previous sections for inspiration.

- Be patient and pay attention to detail as you weave the intricate patterns. Take breaks to assess your progress and make any necessary adjustments.

7. Continue weaving:

- Keep repeating step 6, adding layers of intricate patterns around the central motif, until your bracelet reaches the desired length.

- You can adjust the number of layers and the complexity of the patterns based on your preference.

8. Finish the bracelet:

- Once you've reached the desired length, tie a knot at the end of the last row to secure the weaving.

- Trim any excess cord or floss, leaving a small tail.

- You can add clasps, braided ends, or additional knots to finish the bracelet, depending on your preference.

Creating a complex pattern, such as a diamond or star design, requires patience, practice, and attention to detail. Enjoy the process of weaving the intricate patterns and admire the beautiful results of your craftsmanship.

- Tips for tackling advanced patterns and troubleshooting common challenges.

When tackling advanced friendship bracelet patterns, it's important to approach them with patience, practice, and a willingness to learn. Here are some tips to help you navigate advanced patterns and troubleshoot common challenges:

1. Familiarize yourself with the pattern: Take the time to thoroughly read and understand the pattern instructions before you begin. Pay attention to any specific techniques or knotting sequences mentioned.

2. Start with simpler variations: If the advanced pattern seems daunting, consider practicing with simpler variations or smaller sections of the pattern first. This will help you build your confidence and master the techniques involved.

3. Break it down into sections: Complex patterns can often be broken down into smaller sections or repeating elements. Focus on one section at a time, ensuring you understand and master each section before moving on to the next. This approach can make the pattern more manageable and less overwhelming.

4. Practice the individual knots: If the pattern introduces new knotting

techniques, take the time to practice them separately before incorporating them into the pattern. Practice the knots on a small piece of cord or thread to familiarize yourself with the technique and achieve consistency.

5. Use visual aids and resources: Utilize visual aids such as diagrams, video tutorials, or online resources that demonstrate the advanced pattern or techniques involved. Visual references can provide clarity and help you better understand the steps involved.

6. Take your time and be patient: Advanced patterns require precision and attention to detail. Take your time with each knot and ensure it is executed

correctly before moving on. Rushing can lead to mistakes and inconsistencies in the pattern.

7. Maintain consistent tension: Consistent tension is crucial for achieving a neat and professional-looking bracelet. Pay attention to the tension of your knots throughout the pattern to ensure they are neither too tight nor too loose.

8. Use contrasting colors for clarity: When working on complex patterns with multiple elements, consider using contrasting colors for different sections or layers. This will make it easier to differentiate between the elements and follow the pattern instructions accurately.

9. Keep a clean working area: Organize your materials and keep your working area clean and free from distractions. This will help you stay focused and avoid mistakes.

10. Troubleshoot as you go: If you encounter challenges or make mistakes, don't get discouraged. Take the time to analyze the issue and troubleshoot it. Sometimes unraveling a few knots or undoing a section can help you correct errors and continue with the pattern.

Remember, advanced patterns require practice and perseverance. Don't be afraid to make mistakes as they are an opportunity to learn and improve. With time and practice, you'll develop the skills and confidence to tackle even the most intricate friendship bracelet patterns.

Conclusion:

11.3 Reflecting on the joy and satisfaction of creating unique friendship bracelets.

Creating unique friendship bracelets brings a sense of joy, satisfaction, and fulfillment. Here are some reflections on the experience:

1. **Expressing creativity:** Friendship bracelets allow us to unleash our creativity and create something truly unique. We have the freedom to choose colors, patterns, and designs that reflect our personal style and the recipient's preferences. The process of designing and weaving the bracelets allows us to

express ourselves artistically and create wearable works of art.

2. Personalized gifts: Friendship bracelets are not just beautiful accessories; they also carry sentimental value. Weaving a bracelet for a friend or loved one shows thoughtfulness and care. The time and effort invested in creating a bracelet specifically tailored to their taste and personality make it a meaningful and personalized gift that can strengthen the bond between friends.

3. Mindful and meditative practice: Creating friendship bracelets can be a meditative and calming activity. As we focus on the rhythmic weaving and knotting, our minds can quiet down and find a sense of peace. The repetitive nature of the process allows us to be fully present in the moment, promoting mindfulness and relaxation.

4. Sense of accomplishment: Completing a friendship bracelet brings a deep sense of accomplishment. Seeing the final result of our efforts, whether it's a simple design or an intricate pattern, fills us with pride and satisfaction. Knowing that we have created something beautiful and meaningful with our own hands boosts our confidence and encourages us to continue exploring our creativity.

5. Meaningful connections: Friendship bracelets have a long-standing tradition of symbolizing love, friendship, and unity. When we gift a handmade bracelet, we not only give a tangible item but also a piece of ourselves and our connection to the recipient. It serves as a reminder of the special bond we share and the memories we've created together.

6. Positive impact on well-being: Engaging in creative activities like making friendship bracelets has been linked to improved well-being. It provides a sense of purpose, fulfillment, and relaxation. It can also serve as a healthy outlet for stress and a way to disconnect from the demands of daily life.

7. Building a sense of community: The art of friendship bracelet making has a widespread following, with communities of crafters sharing their creations, patterns, and tips. Engaging with this community allows us to connect with like-minded individuals, exchange ideas, and inspire one another. The shared love for friendship bracelets can foster a sense of belonging and camaraderie.

Creating unique friendship bracelets is a delightful and rewarding endeavor. It allows us to tap into our creativity, share meaningful gifts, find inner peace, and connect with others. Whether we make them for ourselves or for our loved ones, the process and outcome bring immense joy and satisfaction, making friendship bracelet making a cherished and enduring craft.

11.4 Encouragement to continue exploring new patterns, techniques, and personalizations.

I encourage you to continue your journey of exploring new patterns, techniques, and personalizations in friendship bracelet making. The world of friendship bracelets is vast and filled with endless possibilities. Here's some encouragement to inspire your ongoing exploration:

1. Embrace curiosity: Approach each new pattern or technique with curiosity and a willingness to learn. Be open to trying new ideas, experimenting with different color combinations, and pushing the boundaries of your creativity. Embracing curiosity allows you to discover unique designs and techniques that make your friendship bracelets truly one-of-a-kind.

2. Challenge yourself: Don't be afraid to step outside of your comfort zone and take on more intricate patterns or advanced techniques. Pushing yourself to learn and master new skills will not only expand your repertoire but also boost your confidence in your abilities. Remember that with practice and perseverance, you can tackle even the most complex patterns.

3. Personalize with meaning: Infuse your friendship bracelets with personal touches and meaning. Incorporate symbols, initials, or meaningful colors that hold significance for you and the recipient. Personalizing your bracelets adds an extra layer of sentiment and makes them truly special.

4. Share and inspire: Share your creations with others, whether it's gifting them to friends or showcasing them online. By sharing your work, you inspire and encourage others to explore their own creativity. Engage with the friendship bracelet community, exchange ideas, and learn from fellow crafters. Collaborating and sharing experiences can lead to new discoveries and inspire fresh ideas.

5. Document your journey: Keep a journal or a visual diary of your friendship bracelet creations. Take notes on the patterns you've tried, the techniques you've learned, and the color combinations you've experimented with. This not only helps you track your progress but also serves as a source of inspiration for future projects.

6. Attend workshops or join classes: Consider attending workshops or joining classes dedicated to friendship bracelet making. These can provide you with valuable insights, guidance from experienced instructors, and the opportunity to connect with other enthusiasts. Learning from experts and collaborating with fellow learners can expand your skills and inspire you to explore new horizons.

7. Stay connected with trends: Keep an eye on current trends and popular techniques in friendship bracelet making. Follow blogs, social media accounts, and websites dedicated to the craft. Staying connected with the community and being aware of emerging trends can give you fresh ideas and keep your creativity flowing.

Remember, the joy of friendship bracelet making lies in the process of exploration and self-expression. Each pattern, technique, and personalization you discover adds depth and excitement to your craft. So, embrace the journey, let your creativity soar, and continue to create beautiful friendship bracelets that reflect your unique style and creativity.

11.5 Final thoughts on the meaningful connections fostered through the exchange of friendship bracelets.

In the world of friendship bracelets, there is something truly special about the meaningful connections that are fostered through the exchange of these handmade tokens of love and friendship. Here are some final thoughts on the significance of these connections:

1. Symbol of love and friendship: Friendship bracelets have long been recognized as symbols of love, friendship, and unity. When we give or receive a friendship bracelet, we are acknowledging the importance of the bond we share with another person. It serves as a tangible reminder of the affection, support, and connection we have with them.

2. Cultivating relationships: The act of creating and exchanging friendship bracelets is an opportunity to strengthen relationships and deepen connections. Whether it's between friends, family members, or romantic partners, the process of making and sharing these bracelets allows us to invest time, effort, and thoughtfulness into the relationship. It can spark conversations, create shared memories, and strengthen the emotional bonds we have with one another.

3. Expressing care and appreciation: Friendship bracelets are heartfelt gifts that convey care, appreciation, and thoughtfulness. They show that we have taken the time to create something unique and meaningful for someone we care about. By exchanging friendship bracelets, we are expressing our love, gratitude, and support, and reminding the recipient that they hold a special place in our hearts.

4. Cross-cultural connections: Friendship bracelets have a universal appeal that transcends borders and cultures. They are found in various traditions and have been exchanged by people around the world for centuries. This shared practice creates an opportunity for cross-cultural connections and understanding. By embracing and sharing the art of friendship bracelet making, we can bridge cultural divides and celebrate the common threads that bind us together.

5. Acts of kindness and positivity: The act of giving a friendship bracelet is an act of kindness and positivity. It spreads joy, warmth, and happiness to both the giver and the receiver. It is a simple yet powerful gesture that can brighten someone's day, uplift their spirits, and remind them of the beauty and goodness in the world.

6. Building a sense of community: Friendship bracelet making has created a vibrant and inclusive community of crafters, enthusiasts, and artists. Engaging with this community allows us to connect with like-minded individuals, share our creations, exchange ideas, and inspire one another. The sense of belonging and camaraderie within this community is a testament to the power of friendship bracelets in bringing people together.

7. Lasting memories: Friendship bracelets have the ability to create lasting memories. They become treasured keepsakes that remind us of the moments and relationships that have shaped our lives. Years later, we can look back at the friendship bracelets we've given or received and recall the stories, emotions, and connections they represent.

In a world that often feels fast-paced and disconnected, friendship bracelets serve as gentle reminders of the beauty of human connection, love, and friendship. They have the power to create moments of joy, deepen relationships, and foster a sense of belonging. So, embrace the opportunity to exchange friendship bracelets, celebrate the connections in your life, and spread love and positivity through this timeless and cherished tradition.

Printed in Great Britain
by Amazon

42543677R00116